Daily Breakfast Recipes

Asha Rani Vohra

V&S PUBLISHERS

Published by:

V&S PUBLISHERS

F-2/16, Ansari road, Daryaganj, New Delhi-110002
☎ 23240026, 23240027 • *Fax:* 011-23240028
Email: info@vspublishers.com • *Website:* www.vspublishers.com

Regional Office : Hyderabad
5-1-707/1, Brij Bhawan (Beside Central Bank of India Lane)
Bank Street, Koti, Hyderabad - 500 095
☎ 040-24737290
E-mail: vspublishershyd@gmail.com

Branch Office : Mumbai
Jaywant Industrial Estate, 1st Floor–108, Tardeo Road
Opposite Sobo Central Mall, Mumbai – 400 034
☎ 022-23510736
E-mail: vspublishersmum@gmail.com

Follow us on:

© **Copyright:** *V&S PUBLISHERS*
Edition 2018

CONTENTS

Publisher's Note

The Indian housewife today is no longer the same as she was in the bygone days, who spent half of her life working in the kitchen with a back bent. Except for cooking, women of olden age living in the interior of their houses had no direct connection with their guests and almost no ambition in life.

Now she is a conscious housewife or a working woman, useful for the society. Progress in science and technology has made her world trouble-free. She herself wants to move with the times. She wishes to do her work better with the help of scientific equipments, technological ways and means, and gives her work an artistic touch, thus saving her labour and time which can be utilised further for other useful purposes. Such a training includes essential knowledge about food, efficient running of the kitchen and looking after it properly, cleanliness while cooking and serving food artistically, welcoming of guests and all modern etiquettes pertaining to it.

There are other books on culinary art and recipes available in the market. But this book is different from them.

An attempt has been made to cater to the metropolitan as well as the small town housewives. They face day to day problems about what to serve for breakfast, or how to serve it, so that the family gets proper nourishment, and also to provide a tasteful angle to their likings.

The book *Daily Breakfast Recipe* contains recipes with their ingredients and methods of preparation, special tip-offs and all the exclusive characteristics as mentioned above.

A Language of The Plates

"She cooks beautifully …she is so clean and efficient in her cooking…she serves in such a pleasing manner that one feels like praising her to the skies. There seems to be some magic in her hands."

You must have been showered with such praises now and then and felt elated about them.

Taste of food and its attractive presentation– in other words pleasure of the palate and feast for the eyes- are at par, as far as eating goes. Food may be very palatable, nutritious, but if its presentation is not such that it can speak out to the eater, then all the money and labour spent on it becomes meaningless. Satisfaction from eating should be accompanied by a language.

You may be very good at cooking. The quality of cooking, eye on neatness and cleanliness while cooking, correct method of cooking to preserve the food values, coupled with the tastes of the eaters, breaking of monotony in the menu, and above all, an attractive way of serving – all these combine to speak of your culinary art.

This book is different from other cookery books, being devoted to the art of presenting food in a way which pleases the eyes, along with the recipes of some new and special dishes. Emphasis is on the recipes of a few selected dishes, along with suggestions about serving them attractively – every item has been substantiated by a picture.

Due to the developments in the field of science and technology, there are innumerable special dishes in an Indian menu. It is not possible to include all these recipes in a small pictorial book. But some nutritious and delicious dishes have been incorporated, Methods for serving them attractively are also given along with the ingredients and the cooking style.

These are mere suggestions, because the same dish can be cooked and served in various artistic ways. With this belief in mind, the book is dedicated and presented to you. Hope it serves its purpose to enlighten the cook in you. Try out the new and interesting recipes given in the book. *Enjoy cooking and enjoy eating*!

ART OF COOKING

*I*n a modern society, stress is laid on how the food tastes as well as how it is presented. So every young lady these days is keen to learn this art through cookery classes in domestic science courses, books, magazines and periodicals.

In Indian homes, sitting on a wooden stool or plank or floor, eating in metal plates and sitting on a chair and eating on a dining table, are prevalent side by side. But eating in the kitchen is confined within the family and eating at a table sitting on a chair is preferred when the guests have to be entertained. Now in urban life, eating on dining table is becoming more popular day by day in almost every home and the old custom of feeding the guests seated on the floor is almost extinct.

Ancient Indian Custom

Due to lack of space, if feeding a large number of guests on the floor is convenient to you, first of all, clean the floor thoroughly. Then spread druggets or mats in long rows and place wooden stools in front. If guests are too many in number and you are short of stools, use wooden planks instead. Cover them with clean white sheets. If that also is not possible, you may place the plates on the floor with *Alpana* or *Rangoli* designs. Flowers also may be used to decorate the place. If the food is to be served on leaf plates or plantain leaves, they should be cleaned thoroughly.

If the food is served on plates, put as much of it as can be consumed, so that there is no wastage in these days of soaring prices. You may serve more than once, but do not force food on your guests or serve them even after they say no. Your art of serving will be judged by how efficiently you serve the food on a plate, how you serve the further helping, how warm your behaviour is while welcoming guests and also how you have decorated the place.

So this art of hosting and serving has also to be taken care of, besides cooking attractive and palatable dishes.

Modern Method

These days most of the households do not have so many stools or planks and the above kind of entertaining is not in vogue. The Western style of eating on table and chair has become a part and parcel of our lives now. Taking note of the changing times and also convenience, there is no harm in adopting it. These days training in the art of serving is based on this method. So it is necessary to learn and imbibe it in your day to day cooking.

Tip off

In ancient Indian custom, the food used to be served on the floor in the kitchen. This was like an open kitchen of the modern times.

A modern kitchen has facilities for cooking while standing. This avoids getting up every time a thing is needed. No bending either. This way food can be cooked faster and more conveniently. It is less tiring, rather energy conserving, dress does not get muffled up and no fear of fire with children around. So, a kitchen should be planned with shelves all around and a table or a platform should be there for cooking in standing position. Have closed cabinets instead of open shelves for storage and a cupboard with iron mesh to keep milk, curd, vegetables etc., in case you do not have a refrigerator. This will add to cleanliness and comfort in the kitchen. Slabs made of concrete, chips or cement should be against two walls and two and a half feet above the ground.

Place the stove, or gas burner or cooking range on one side and all other necessary things in the closed cabinets below the platform or on the wall. Since everything will be handy this way, work will be easier and less time consuming. Place a deep sink for washing utensils on the other side of the wall, or in the centre, or in a corner. The tap should be on top and proper arrangements should be made for the flow of water. Make a mesh cabinet with a rack to keep washed plates on the upper part. Rest of the utensils can be kept on a slanting, narrow plank near the sink, for the water to drain out easily.

There should be some vacant space nearby, to be used for chopping vegetables, kneading flour and such jobs. Things to be used for these may be kept in a cabinet and cleaned properly for a healthy and hygienic cooking. There should also be adequate ventilation in the kitchen, so an exhaust fan or a chimney is a must.

Tip off

A kitchen equipped with all amenities is like a modern car of today equipped with all the latest gadgets. Isn't it?

THE IDEAL KITCHEN

CLEANLINESS

*y*our family's health depends on the cleanliness of your kitchen and your convenience while cooking depends on how well equipped your kitchen is. Hence, equal attention should be paid to both these aspects.

Arrangement for proper light and air in the kitchen is essential along with the rest of the décor. There should be a window in front of the door for cross ventilation and the platform for cooking should be a little away from it. Water outlet if not adequate can result in the floor well becoming full of dirt and a breeding ground for germs. Walls and roof should be whitewashed once or twice a year. Walls should not be infested with cobwebs.

Clean the shelves and the floor after every meal. Add insecticides once or twice a week in the water used for sweeping the floor.

Scrub the place used for washing utensils with any detergent and a brush. In case there is no proper drainage of water from washed utensils, fix a sheet of aluminium or rubber there and add a small spoon of ammonia in the water used for cleaning the kitchen platform. This will remove greasiness. Doors and windows of the kitchen should have iron mesh, to prevent flies from entering. The garbage tin should have a lid. Burn waste paper once a week in the empty metal bin to avoid the danger of catching germs.

Change the dusters of the kitchen frequently and wash them with antiseptic soap or any detergent. Keep all the food items always covered. With such care, there will be no fear of contracting diseases. Cleanliness of the kitchen is absolutely essential for you and your family's health.

Tip off

Sunlight and fresh air kill germs. Arrange for proper ventilation in your kitchen, by providing it with an exhaust or chimney.

All women cook at homes and even men are good cooks, these days. So it is not necessary to tell them the basics. The most important question is whether the food prepared has a thought behind it, or is it done casually? Are the nutritional values kept intact scientifically, or emphasis is only on taste? Are factors like saving of time, labour and money taken into account while cooking or half of one's life is spent fretting and fuming while working in the kitchen. It is important to give a thought to all these. For efficient cooking, the following tips may be kept in mind.

Keep all necessary things handy and keep them at their proper places after use, so that you do not waste time looking for them again and again.

Use double burner gas stove, or a cooking range for your convenience and faster cooking.

Mechanical Gadgets

To save labour, invest money in mechanical gadgets once. Such an investment pays in the long run. Save money out of your entertainment budget, or spend a little less on clothes and equip yourself with some gadgets like gas, heater, cooker, toaster, immersion rod for hot water, mixie, oven, etc. Besides these, having a fridge in the kitchen is convenient. Things like

geyser can wait. If none of these can be obtained, get at least a stove, cooker and an icebox for yourself. Similarly, if the kitchen is not conveniently built or renovation is not possible, get a big table made. Below the table, closed cabinet on one side and mesh cabinet on the other side may be made for storage. A stone slab or metal sheet can be placed on the top, where the gas or stove is kept. You will gain by saving time and buy the convenience.

Keep a special eye on cleanliness and tidiness while cooking. Everything should be covered. Your hands and dusters should be clean. Do not spill water and scatter garbage all around. Their places should be properly specified.

Arrange all the necessary things before lighting the burner for cooking so that there is no wastage of fuel, oil, gas and electricity.

Cook Well

Wash the vegetables before chopping. They lose their mineral salts if washed afterwards. Green leafy vegetables should be definitely washed before chopping. While cooking, care should be taken that the nutritive value and natural taste is not lost in the process. Cook vegetables in steam. If it is necessary to drain water after boiling, use this water in *dal* or cooking pulses. Do not throw away the starchy rice water after draining. Use enough water to cook rice, which gets absorbed during cooking. This way vegetables and rice will not lose their nutritive value. If cottage cheese (paneer) is made at home, use its water in *dal* and vegetables. Clean the wheat well before grinding. Do not sift the wheat flour. You will lose vitamins E and B with the remnants. Whole pulses (*dals*) should be used as far as possible.

Cooking on a high flame harms food values resulting in the loss of vitamins. Most of the food can be cooked on low or medium fire. Food values remain intact if the food is cooked in cookers.

Cook soft vegetables with skin. Cook them in steam or boil them. Some vegetables can be eaten raw. If you prefer vegetables fried in ghee, do not use too much spices. Fry them enough, so that their juices do not burn out.

One should be energetic and attentive while cooking. Cleanliness, saving time and labour, efficiency, all have their importance. You may utilize the extra time saved for some other purpose. Wash your hands well and use a little moisturizer or hand cream after your cooking is over. Take care of your hands and get the nails manicured once a week or fortnightly, so that the stains of vegetables and dirt after washing do not show in the cracks of your hands. It is absolutely essential to keep the nails clean.

So, keeping the nutritive values of food intact while cooking, saving of time, labour and fuel, cleanliness and neatness – all these combined together make for a scientific and technical way of cooking.

Tip off

Few extra things helpful in cleanliness and safety:

➤ Burnol
➤ Hand lotion
➤ Hand cream
➤ Soap, Vim
➤ Brush for cleaning bottles
➤ A piece of sponge to clean the sink and buckets
➤ Mop to sweep the floor
➤ Two hand towels – one near the sink and the other in the kitchen for wiping hands
➤ Napkin
➤ A low wooden plank, for standing on it while using an electric heater

*D*elicious food may not seem palatable if it is not served properly. So the art of serving and table decoration is as important as the culinary art itself.

If you have a separate dining room, it should be well ventilated and lighted. Paint the walls with colours pleasing to the eyes. Put bright curtains, but the colour should not be too dark. The lampshades should have pretty colours and the bulbs should not be very bright during dinner. These days candle light dinners are highly appreciated. A beautiful candle stand can be used for this purpose, or a dimly lit chandelier can be hung from the ceiling.

If there is no separate dining room, the *verandah* adjacent to the kitchen can be enclosed, decorated and converted into a small dining room. Otherwise place the dining table and chairs on one side of your living room. If the living room is longish, a different colour or a standing screen partition can be put in the middle, to give this portion the look of a separate room.

If your living room is small and separate dining area cannot be carved out of it, use a small folding table. Put it on one side of the room and expand it, when necessary, to be used as a dining table A few chairs and puffies, etc. can be put around it . The multi-purpose folding table can be used as a centre table also. Four to six people can use it together at a time conveniently.

Decoration of the Dining Table

While writing about the decoration of the dining table, we assume that you have table with atleast four to six chairs around it. If arrangements have to be made for large number of guests, many such tables can be put in an open space. They can be hired. It is evident that such an arrangement is necessary only for big formal parties or functions. A few guests frequenting your home can be entertained on your dining table.

Cover this table with clean, washed, ironed white sheet. Then arrange artistically embroidered or painted table mats on it. One set of mats has 13 pieces – 1 big long mat to place the serving bowls in the centre, six middle sized mats for plates and six small mats for side plates. Arrange them in such a way that in front of every chair, the middle sized mat is on the right and the small is on the left of them. They should be placed side by side.

Now place big and small plates on them in the same order. Put glasses on the right side, on the upper side of the big plate. Put two spoons on the right side of each plate. If soup is to be served, a big soup spoon should also be provided. Tablespoons should be used for eating rice. If knives and forks are to be used for eating, these also should be placed in an organized way. So put small and big spoons, fork and knife together, near each plate and put a napkin too. Decorate the centre or around the serving bowls with flower arrangements on the table. Whether you use a bouquet of flowers or decorate the table in the Ikebana style or with Rangoli, depends on your own good taste and sense. Salt and pepper cellars, bottles of sauce, *chutney* and pickles should be arranged neatly between the serving bowls.

Decorating Napkins on the Table

Make napkins out of thick cotton material. White, light pink or lemon coloured materials can be used. They should be absolutely clean, washed, starched and ironed. Fold them into eight squares or triangles and place them on the big plates, or shape them into flowers and place them in the empty glasses. They may be folded like caps or boats and kept on the table. This art is an important part of table decoration and must be learnt.

A Few More Designs For You to Learn

1.   Napkin flowers in the glasses placed on a long table, can be made thus:

Hold the lower edge of the napkin with four folds. Fold the edge a bit and stick it in the glass. Now out of the four folds lower the two on the side and shape like two open leaves by bringing the four folds lower the two on the side and shape like two open leaves by bringing the pointed edges in front. Now open the centre leaves opposite to each other. It will look like a *blossoming flower*. It is easy to do it, if the napkin is well starched.

2.   There are more methods of decorating napkins.

To make this design, double up 4-fold napkin from the centre. Make a triangle and turn the lower portion upside down as shown in the photograph. Now keep it on the plate or near it. Place it upside down. It looks beautiful.

3.   To make a design that looks like the cap of a waiter:

Fold the napkin into eight and turn two folds in one direction and two in the opposite direction fixing the two edges to each other. When opened, it will be a boat like cap. Place it on the plate or near it.

4.   The design in the centre is made with two napkins:

Spread a doubly folded napkin. Then gather the whole napkin, like saree folds. Double it from the lower edge and fix in the glass. It will look like an open fan. This single design can be used. To make the other design shown here, fold another napkin starting from one corner. Fold it double and fix in the glass. The back side should be seen from the rear part of the first napkin and the front should be below the fan. Turn the face in front and open it a bit. There will be a dancing peacock in the glass. Napkins can be decorated in many ways. You may experiment with new designs. Guests open up these napkins to spread on their knees, after they sit down to eat. Before that, these napkins add to the beauty of the table.

Sweet dishes can be decorated in many ways with chopped almonds, pistachio, cherries, silver wrapping, cardamom powder, saffron, etc. You can decorate a plate according to the festival, function and occasion. Here you have to show your entire artistic talent.

Sweets can also be decorated in a special way on Diwali for the entire family. Mango leaves and a coconut can be placed on the auspicious pot. Fruits are decorated on a plantain Rangoli design around them and lighted lamps on mats with Batik designs add to the beauty.

If you invite a newly married couple for a meal, a different kind of decoration on the dining table can present a light humour, along with an important piece of advice. The whole atmosphere is bound to become cheerful. You can make four figures made out of boiled potatoes of a man woman, a boy and a girl and decorate them with cloves (eyes), cardamom powder (clothes, etc.) tomato rings (caps) and cabbage leaves (veil). Black pepper powder can be used instead of cardamom for this salad.

Similarly cartoons, dolls, birds, animals, Santa Claus, boy doll and girl doll, etc. can be made out of potatoes, thickened milk and other ingredients for a children's party. The party will be more enjoyable for children and the guests will be delighted. You will be showered with praises.

But decoration of food preparations should not be given importance only on special occasions or parties. You should incorporate this art in your daily life too to make your food more attractive and alluring. Decorate dishes of vegetables, salads, rice plate, custard, pudding, etc. Salad decorations should be experimented with, every day. A separate chapter has been devoted to it in the coming pages. Decorate the sweet dishes with cardamom, chopped dry fruits, cherries, raisins, cashew, wrapping, pieces of fruits, icing, etc. and the salty dishes with chopped coriander, green chillies, tomato, beetroot, onion rings, carrot, flowers of radish, mint leaves, etc., They will enhance the pleasure of eating and look very interesting.

Great stress has been laid in this book on the decoration aspect, encouraging girls and boys to learn this art along with the culinary art. Provide proper cutlery for serving preparations decorated with spices, dry fruits, etc., like tongs to hold, serving spoon, small spoon, fork, spatula, etc. Put them in order and do concentrate on other things also, like decorating candles, Ikebana, money plant, some show pieces appropriate for the occasion.

The most important aspect is to make a habit of using this art and developing it by giving a new shape to it every day with the help of your novel ideas and experiments.

- If an oven is not available, bake on coal fire. Place big burning pieces of coal in the lower section of the burner (angeethee). Put a tin sheet or a lid on top of the burner. Place a cake tin on it. Put a vessel up-side down on the cake tin and put a few burning pieces of coal on it. Cake will be baked just as in an oven.

- While roasting in an oven, place the food stuff in a vessel with one inch high sides. Gravy will not spill from this vessel. While frying meat, fill three-fourths of a bowl with water and place it in the oven. This will prevent meat from burning and ensure proper cooking.

- While shopping for good quality meat, fish and chicken, keep the following in mind. Fresh meat of goat or lamb will have firm and white fat. While the colour of tender meat will be a mixture of blue and pink and the broken bone in it will be of white colour. Old animal's meat will be a mixture of dark blue and pink and edge of a bone will be red. Do not buy light mauve coloured meat with yellow fat. It is generally stale. If a bird is healthy, its chest should be firm with soft edges of bone. Infirm chest and hard edges of bone belong to an old bird. Fresh fish has life like bright eyes and it smells good. Fish with socketed dead eyes is stale. Its smell is also different.

- To test the freshness of an egg, put it in a vessel with water. If it is fresh, it will remain there in a slanting position. Rotten eggs stand erect in water. If the egg has gone absolutely bad, it will stand erect on its pointed end on the surface of the vessel.

- Fruits and vegetables reveal themselves by touch and smell. Do not buy half ripe, overripe and spoiled fruits. Do not buy off season vegetables and also whithered or broken vegetables and fruits. If the vegetables are to be stored for a long time without refrigeration, wet them and wrap them in a sheet of paper. Fold the paper from all sides, preventing the passage of air through the vegetables. Fruits remain fresh for a longer time, if its stem is coated with wax.

- While buying canned food stuff, see to it that the can is not dented or swollen from any side.

- If a broken egg is to be poached in boiling water, add a spoon of vinegar in the water. This will keep the egg in shape.

- Before making an omelette, brush the frying pan with a pinch of salt, then put the ghee, oil or butter.

- Before beating an egg in a bowl, wet it a bit. The egg won't stick to the bowl. Before extracting juice from a lime, soak it in hot water for a while. The quantity of juice will be more.
- While cooking rice, add a few drops of lime juice to it. Rice will be whiter with separated grains.
- Add a few drops of lime juice while cooking apples also. This will prevent the apples from turning black.
- Boil water before boiling vegetables. Then gradually add vegetables to it in small quantities.
- A pinch of salt added to the water preserves the natural colouring of these vegetables. Root vegetables should be cooked in a closed vessel, on low fire, while green vegetables should be cooked in an open vessel.
- Add piece of cottage cheese (paneer) to onion soup for better taste.
- If the eggs get overboiled leave them in cold water before peeling.
- If a vegetable preparation becomes too salty, make a small ball out of the wheat dough, soak it in the gravy and remove. If the dish becomes too hot with chillies, add a few drops of lime juice to it. Care should be taken to check on all these before serving the food.
- If the juice of a lime or any other citrus fruit is to be added to any milk preparation for taste, add it drop by drop. This will prevent milk from curdling.
- If deeper red colour is preferred for gravy, do not add too much chillie, but take out the seeds from two whole red chillies, soak them in water for half an hour, add a little vinegar to it, squeeze the chillies and add this water to the gravy. The colour will be deep red.
- If hard raw meat is to be made tender, rub lime on it, or wrap it up in banana leaves.
- If bread gets dry, steam it for some time.
- Add more oil and less vinegar to a salad dressing and mix well.
- Add sour flavouring to vegetables only when they are three-fourth cooked, not earlier.
- If ghee is to be added to pastries in place of butter, let it cool before adding the ghee.
- Fried things should be placed on absorbent paper before transferring them on a serving plate or dish.

Tip off

The Menu should be planned for your family as well as for your guests beforehand. If you haven't been following this, try and cultivate this habit for your family as well.

*T*he dining table should be used for family bonding, not for crossing swords over unappetizing dishes.

Your family's daily menu should be planned according to your family members' tastes, their health and needs of individual members. Hard and fast rules cannot be laid down for daily eating, as for special and formal occasions. Neither can the food habits of the family be altered completely. Even then a few general tips should be kept in mind.

Plan lunch, dinner, breakfast and evening tea in such a way that they provide all the nutrition necessary for a day. At the same time, they should not be monotonous. All the meals should have variety. They should be good to eat and balanced too.

Offer Variety

To keep this balance, try to alter the menu every day. Whole week's diet should be balanced in such a way that it provides all that a body needs and at the same time pleases every member of the family by its variety. Choice and necessity of children, adults, women, men, elders, etc. should be incorporated in your menu.

Include one dry and one dish with gravy in the daily menu. If one is heavy, the other should be easily digestible. If one is soft the other should be chewable. That is absolutely essential to activate your teeth. One meal in a day should be simple and light. The other meal could be a little heavy and elaborate. This depends on the convenience of the family. Those going to school, college and office should eat a light lunch and their dinner could be heavier. But it should not be taken too late at night. Those used to taking dinner late should keep it light and lunch could be a full meal. By and large, it is better to follow this rule for a healthy living. Exceptions of course, could be there once in a while.

Make it a habit to serve food in an attractive way. Special decors could be used for special occasions. But the family should not be neglected also. As far as serving of food is concerned, cleanliness and nutrition go with health. Similarly, the art of presenting food plays an important part in mental happiness. Good food not served in an attractive manner

Daily Breakfast Recipes | 25

will kill the appetite and even if the food is not good and tasty but presented in a pleasant way will enhance your appetite. The joy of eating well served food has its effect on the digestive system.

Serve Well

If you want that family members should give up fried, spicy food and take to dishes that are healthy but less palatable, like salads, you have to give special attention to the art of serving. Clean, presentable serving bowls, shining plates, well presented food on these plates, their colour coordination, flower arrangement on the table, properly laid napkins, spoons, etc. and a smiling face of the hostess will certainly attract everybody towards the dining table.

Learn new methods of serving and decorating and keep changing them as you learn new recipes. Your will win everybody's heart and it will help the atmosphere at home remain fresh and lively. Just try it out.

On a holiday, plan one menu like a family feast. Satisfaction, taste and enjoyment should be given priority with of course, healthy food items, such as vegetables and fruits. The meal can be enjoyed together in this way as the joy of a family lunch/dinner has its own part to play in building up your health and keeping you happy.

Tip off

A family that eats healthy food together stays together and remains healthy and cheerful.

$\mathcal{G}$uests are welcome in every home. Extending hospitality to the guests is a distinctive part of the great Indian tradition. With changing social and economic conditions, this particular tradition has become a little obscure no doubt, but it has not been wiped out completely, as it happens to be an integral part of our lives.

Adjustments within the existing conditions is a special quality found in most of the Indians. On one hand, they have coped with problems like inflation, scarcity and non-availability of food stuffs and on the other hand, they have incorporated different kinds of delicacies from various states within the country and abroad also, in their eating. With this, there have been remarkable changes in their eating habits and modes of serving food. The adjustments to bring about these changes have indeed been wonderful.

Indian Hospitality

How much labour, money and time is to be spent on looking after the guests depends entirely on the household budget and also the time in hand for a working or stay at home housewife. But *hospitality is a must for every household*. A point worth mentioning here is that though the labour, time and money saving devices are indeed highly developed yet at the same time more attention is being paid to learning special food preparations and to present them in an attractive fashion. All women's magazines carry columns on cookery and young girls show genuine interest in joining cookery classes. The younger generation not only learns to make new food preparations through these cookery columns and classes, but also the art of serving them, and get trained in throwing parties on their own. Such training has been accepted as a part of modern living.

So it is evident that the Indian hospitality has not deteriorated, in spite of many circumstantial setbacks. It has only been moulded according to times, with the help of science and technology. Whether the guests come unannounced or they are invitees on a special occasion; whether the meeting is in a club or a restaurant, or at a specially arranged party, every young lady these days has to know the art of entertaining.

The training imparted in this art may be divided into four parts:

➤ Food cooked should be clean, proper and tasty.

➤ Family's daily necessities and tastes should be taken care of.

➤ As a guest, proper etiquette should be maintained.

➤ Be pleasant as a hostess.

*I*f you do not live in a village and are a part of the urban population, your social sphere is bound to be wide. You may not be visiting clubs, restaurants and parties frequently. But even if you participate in joint functions, parties, some etiquettes and manners have to be observed there too. Lack of knowledge about these may cause embarrassment and create inferiority complex. So it will be advantageous to know the modes of eating-drinking, and conducting oneself on such occasions.

Mixed Culture

Being Indians, we should be proud of our traditions in eating and behaving and we should adopt them in our personal lives. But while mingling with the mixed culture of modern living, it would be in place to conduct oneself according to time, place and atmosphere. For example, if you do not like to use fork and knife for eating, you may keep them aside and eat with your fingers. But if others around are using forks and knives and you would like to be at par with them, you should know the correct way of using forks and knives, otherwise you may become a laughing stock by imitating others in a wrong way. If you are a little watchful, you can get on to the right way by observing others. But it is always better to learn table manners beforehand and learn the etiquette before going to a modern party. Few important tips are given below for your convenience:

➤ When invited to a party, reach there 10 to 15 minutes earlier than the scheduled time. Your reaching too early may cause inconvenience to the host and reaching late will keep others waiting.

➤ If unable to accept an invitation, do inform on the telephone or by writing. Do not forget to thank them for the invitation.

➤ Reach the dining table when requested by the host, not earlier. Your chair should not be too far from the table, or too close to it.

➤ After sitting, unfold the folded or flower like arranged napkin and spread it across your knees to prevent soiling of clothes. This napkin can also be used for wiping hands and mouth.

➤ Do not sit on the chair in a stiff, upright position or bend too much over the table. Do not rest your elbows on the table.

➤ Take part in the discussions going on around you, only if you have a thorough knowledge of the subject. Otherwise just be a silent listener, so that it may not occur to others that everything is Greek to you. It is not good to express nervousness or seem indifferent at such moments. In case you have to attend such parties frequently, the best thing to do would be to increase your general knowledge and try and gain popularity on such occasions. Otherwise be in a pleasant mood, behave and show the good aspects of your nature.

➤ Learn to use fork and knife beforehand or by observing then and there. Handles of your fork and knife should rest on your palms. Press the food with fork and cut it into small bits with the knife. Your knife should be in the right hand and fork in the left. Put the small pieces of food into your mouth with the fork. While pressing the food, the posterior of your knife should be on a higher level. While putting the morsel into the mouth, the lower part should be higher. It will be easier to slice the food if the elbows are kept close to the body.

➤ In a Western meal, soup is served first. A large spoon is provided separately for drinking soup. Soup is to be drunk not from the pointed side of the spoon, but from its sides. Do not make a noise while drinking. Remember, soup is not served again, so do not ask for a second helping.

➤ If you need another helping of any preparation, shift your plate a little in front and give an indication to the bearer. Keep in mind that you will be served from your left side. So when the bearer is on your right, he comes to serve the person sitting on your right.

➤ If you do not like a preparation, avoid taking it. But do not let others know about your dislikes. May be they are liking it and you may spoil their tastes.

➤ If you want to spit out something, put the spoon close to your mouth and take it out on the spoon and keep it on one side of your plate. If something seems unpalatable in the food, leave it in the plate without commenting on it. Your speaking about it may spoil other people's mood.

➤ If the spoon, knife or fork falls on the ground do not pick it up, but ask the bearer to get you another one, or take one from those kept in a corner of the table.

➤ Do not sip tea from the platter. Drink it from the cup. Let the spoon rest on the plate. Do not make a noise while drinking tea or water.

➤ Do not speak with food in your mouth, or laugh loudly while eating. While talking to the person next to you, turn only your neck and not the entire body or chair.

➤ Spoon, knife and fork should not bang against your plate, creating loud noise.

➤ If finger bowls with warm water and lime pieces are provided after the meal, use it for cleaning your fingers. Otherwise go and wash your mouth and hands at the place provided for it. If something gets stuck in between the teeth, use a toothpick to remove it. Keep your left hand in front of your mouth while doing this. If there is no arrangement for washing hands, wipe your mouth with the napkin quietly. Before leaving the table, wait for others too, and don't rush to get out.

➤ In the buffet style of eating, lots of formalities are overlooked. Eatables are kept in large bowls on the table and empty plates and spoons, etc. are put along with them. Pick up the plate and the spoon yourself and serve yourself anything you want, as much as you want. Then come away from the table. Sit and eat if chairs are provided, otherwise eat standing. But do not be totally engrossed in eating. Give importance to meeting people. In a buffet meal, you can move about here and there with the plate in your hand and give company to people you know, while eating.

Tip off

Before leaving, it is most important to praise the food. Speak about the lovely décor in front of your host. Tell him about the good time you had. This is more important than just thanking him. Making complaints or talking of unpleasant things on such occasions are taken as bad manners. If you have something adverse on your mind, do not go to the party. Excuse yourself on some pretext or the other.

*I*f you host a function or a formal party at home, extensive preparations are necessary. Cooking, arranging the house, cleaning, decorating and grooming one self-everything has to be done. To top it all, mounting expenses force the hostess to juggle with her budget.

But nothing can be achieved by showing nervousness, creating a lot of noise and keeping other members of the family on their tenterhooks. Things done in confusion are bound to be full of errors, leading to loss of things and also of time. All this will reflect the immaturity of your mind. On the other hand, things done peacefully, in a planned way, taking care of the budget, etc. will show good results, like everything being done in time, in a proper fashion.

You have to be presentable when the guests arrive.

Your house also has to be in order and neat and clean. It is not possible to achieve all this on the day of the party. A few things can be done a day or two in advance. Some things have to be done the same day. Likewise, some chores have to be done well before the party and others are to be accomplished at the last moment. So make a plan of all that you have to do. Place them in order of priority. Few suggestions are given below for your convenience:

➤ Shampoo your hair one or two days before the party, so that they can be set properly on that day. Washing, shopping and other such chores should be done a day or two in advance, so that no pending work remains to be done on that day.

➤ An evening before the party make a trip to your beautician for facial, pedicure, manicure, etc. Take a long bath well before the party. File your nails and shape your eyebrows also. This will save time to get dressed just before the party and it will also help you to feel and look fresh.

➤ Have a glass of fresh lime in the morning and take a light meal, so that you do not feel sluggish after eating and have enough energy to cope with the work. Brush you teeth thoroughly in the morning.

➤ Choose the dress you will be wearing in the evening and hang it at the proper place. Children's clothes and socks, etc. should also be conveniently placed, so that no time is wasted looking for them.

- Because you will work in the kitchen till late, do not use make-up too early. Complete you work in the kitchen, clean and arrange your house and then devote the last hour to yourself. Use light make-up an hour before the guests arrive.

- Do up yourself and also your house well before the party. Decorate your living room and also the entrance of the house. Rangoli designs, an ethnic pot, wall hangings, Ikebana in a corner, drift wood arrangement, all these will give a special look to the entrance. If it is not possible to use any of these, arrange the flower pots in a special way – in groups or in rows. Flower arrangements on the dining table should be done in the evening.

- If you have a fridge, make a few dishes the previous day and store in the refrigerator. Vegetables, soup, hot snacks, cutlets, *vadas*, etc. should be made fresh on the same day. If the weather is not too hot, a few things can be made earlier, even if there is no facility for storing them in a refrigerator. A few things like desserts, can be bought also, or sweet dish like 'Ras Malai' can be made on the same day in the morning. Fried things like *pakodas* should be freshly made and served hot.

- Some of the fried things like *kachori*, *pakodi*, etc. can be fried earlier and heated up again in ghee before serving. *Bhature-chhole* also can be made earlier and heated up before eating. Things like *puris* and *dosas* should be made absolutely fresh. If you do not have any help for such last moment's chores, hire somebody for that evening, or take the help of a friend or neighbour. Only then you will have time to pay attention to your guests.

- If you do not have any help avoid inviting too many people at a time. Call them for tea instead of a meal. Even then, more than fifteen or twenty guests together may create confusion, especially when the place is small. A small place crowded with too many people is inconvenient for the host and for the guests as well.

- In case you have enough space and a few invitees and two or three people to help you, you may arrange small tables for a tea party or a dinner. Put chairs around these tables, (such parties are more enjoyable outdoors in a garden) or put one single long table, (two tables may be combined to make a large one). Place chairs all around and decorate the table nicely. A bouquet of flowers or ikebana flower arrangement can be placed in the centre. There should be a table mat on the table in front of each chair and plates, spoons, knives, forks and glasses should be placed properly on them. Spread bigger mats in the centre of the table with enough room for serving bowls. Extra things like utensils, plates, etc. should be put on a separate table nerarby, to avoid going to the kitchen repeatedly.

- A hot plate, to warm up food, can be placed on this additional table. Plates for desserts can be placed and arrangements for betel leaves to be taken after meal can also be made on this table. (More details on table decoration given in the following pages.)

➤ If eating is to be in Western style, do not request your guests to eat more. This has to be borne in mind all the time.

➤ Join your guests for the meal, but commence eating with them and not before. Keep your guests company during the meal. Do not finish eating first. This can be embarrassing for your guests and they may hesitate to take fresh helpings.

➤ Keep the atmosphere light and cheerful during the meal. If by chance a mild tiff comes up between two people, try to divert the topic, avoiding offence to any of the guests. Light musical entertainment or mimicry, etc. can be arranged on such occasions.

➤ Lastly, another important thing to be remembered. It very often happens that the hostess looks very presentable. Living and dining rooms, *verandah*, outside, etc. are spick and span, but due to pressure of work, the cleanliness and orderliness of bathroom, kitchen, etc. is thoroughly neglected. This is not right. If any of your guests need to use the bathroom or somebody (specially women) are keen to have peep inside the house, it will not create a good impression. All your outside decoration will seem dull and drab then. Do not show your inefficiency in this manner. After being through with your work, clean up and arrange the kitchen – in fact, the whole house. Ask your domestic help to have a wash after work, wear clean clothes and be ready before the guests arrive.

➤ Guests will praise you after the party and you will apologise for your little shortcomings, politely. Do not mention the hard work you have put in or the tensions you have gone through to make the party a success.

Tip off

Do not send the children out of the house before the party. Instead, teach them social etiquette and good habits.

*I*f your place is small and help is lacking, but at the same time, it is essential to host a dinner or a lunch, arrange a 'buffet' meal. That will be convenient for you. All the food is served in big bowls on one table for everybody to eat together. Full plates and spoons, etc. are placed separately. Guests will stand around the table, pick up their own plates and spoons and serve themselves whatever they want to eat. There is less wastage of food like this and serving everybody individually can also be avoided.

In a 'buffet', you have to pay attention to the following things.

➤ See that the table cloth is spotlessly clean.

➤ Serving bowls should be absolutely clean and sparkling.

➤ Put appropriate serving spoon with every dish on the table.

➤ The food should be hot.

➤ Small bowls or soup plates can be put separately for curd or dessert.

➤ Keep a few empty plates for peeled skin of fruits.

➤ Place one napkin with each plate.

➤ In a buffet meal, paper napkins should be used, to be thrown away later.

➤ Water jug and glasses should be placed on a separate table.

➤ Arrangement should be made for washing hands.

➤ If coffee or tea is to be served, give it hot after the meal – either on the same table or on a separate one, as convenient.

This way of entertaining will be less troublesome for you and your guests will also feel free. But you have to go, find and see to it that all the invitees have eaten well. Pay attention to everybody alike and a little more to those who for some reason had joined others at the table, later.

If there is ample space, rows of chairs can be put a little away from the table, on a side. These chairs can be used by those who prefer to sit and eat. If there is lack of space, people can stand and eat. Soft music in the background helps to make the atmosphere lively.

$\mathcal{Y}$ou do invite your child's friends on his or her birthday. It is an occasion to light candles on a cake, cut it with the strains of 'Happy birthday to you'. You can think of some new ideas, different from the mixed traditions of India and the West. Here are some suggestions for your consideration.

Invite elders only if the child is very small. As soon as they understand the significance of a birthday, invite children of their age group, their friends, so that they feel free to enjoy themselves without the presence of elders. You may include your neighbour's children, even if they are a little younger or older than your child. There will be two gains thus – children in the family and neighbourhood will not feel neglected and secondly, children will not remain confined to their own age group only, but will learn to mix with the younger and older children and also to behave socially. Games to be played before the party can be for the children of the same age group.

Planning the Menu

Your work extends beyond preparing dishes and serving them on each plate for each child. While planning the menu, children's liking must be taken into account. Food should be healthy too. Do not include items like *Chholekulche, Chaat, Mathha* made of flour, *Balushahi*, etc., Decide on things like sweet toasts, juicy sweets made of dried thickened milk, salty puffed rice, fruit cream of ice cream, salty *pakodis* made of *moong, cake, pastries, biscuits, toffees*, etc. Decorate them nicely and arrange them on the table. To enhance the beauty of the party, a few eatables can be included just for decoration or fun. Bird and cock made of dried thickened milk and a joker made with boiled potatoes can also be included just for decorating the table. Boiled eggs in different shapes can also be arranged. Sweet dishes can be garnished with chopped dry fruits, cherries and salty dishes with chopped coriander leaves, grated cottage cheese (paneer), tomato, sauce, etc., to give the dish a different look.

Decorations

Venue of the party should also be decorated according to the children's liking. Have colourful balloons. Arrange photos, cartoons and toys. Caps can be made with coloured papers, golden strips or *Rakhis* kept at home for the children to wear.

Games

Arrange for some games before eating. Have some programmes that will make them laugh. You may think of some light quiz or competition and keep some small prizes for the winners. But such competitions should not give an inferiority complex to any child on a happy occasion. Nobody should feel insulted or ashamed. This has to be borne in mind all the time. It is better to give gifts like toffees, balloons, small toys, picture books, etc., to all the children and some thing extra for the winners.

The most important thing is that you should not confine yourself to the arrangements of the party, alone. You should also not interfere in their games and other entertainments. If the children are enjoying themselves along with the good food, they will cherish the fun of the party for a long time. Your child will also be happy to know that his/her friends had a lovely time and they went back home with pleasant memories of the party. It is unfair to curb the children with words like: "Children, sit quietly, eat silently, do not make noise, etc." This will spoil their fun and mood of the party, as they have come to enjoy and have fun. So without making any nuisance or spoiling any household items – leave them free to play, talk, sing, eat or drink.

Tip off

Children love games and good food. So give them both aplenty and you've won some little loving friends for life.

MOUTH-WATERING RECIPES

Making Tea

A hot cup of tea makes us feel fresh and rejuvenated. It is the first thing in our daily menu.

Tea

Ingredients

5 cups water
5 tsp tea leaves
½ cup boiled milk
sugar (to taste)

Method

➤ Heat water in a kettle. Before boiling, pour a little water in the tea pot to clean and warm it.

➤ When the water in the kettle starts boiling, throw away the water in the tea pot and put 5 teaspoons full of tea leaves in the tea pot. (This is for four people). Usually, it is in the proportion of one spoon for the pot and one spoon per head. If light tea is preferred, lesser tea leaves may be used.

➤ Pour boiling water from the kettle on the tea leaves in the tea pot and close the lid. Then keep aside for a little while. Some people like to stir tea leaves with a spoon. Then pour tea after the tea leaves have settled down on the surface of the kettle.

➤ Tea is ready to be used when tea leaves have settled down. Strain into cups and mix milk and sugar. (Add milk and sugar according to the taste of the drinker).

Tip off

Tea and coffee contain caffeine. We should not drink them in excess.

Making Coffee

Coffee is a favourite beverage of people all over the world.

Coffee

Ingredients

3 cups water
2 tsp instant coffee
1 cup milk
sugar (to taste)

Method

➤ Heat a little water first to clean and warm the coffee pot.

➤ Mix 2 teaspoons full of instant coffee and 4 spoons of milk and beat well.

➤ Boil 3 cups of water with one cup of milk (for four people).

➤ Pour this boiled milk – water in a coffee pot. Stir well with a spoon and keep covered for 2 minutes.

➤ Pour in cups and mix sugar and milk as per taste.

Tip off

Coffee contains antioxidants. It is good for health if taken in moderation.

Nutritious Apple Snack

Instead of serving plain pieces of apple for breakfast, serve them in a different way.

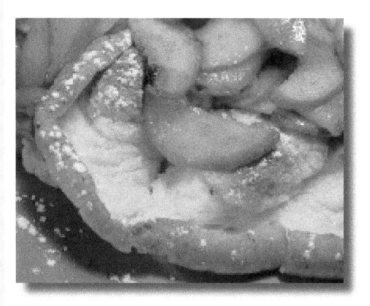

Apple Snack

Ingredients

2 apples
cardamom powder
sugar (to taste)
some milk

Method

Take two apples. Grate one apple coarsely and spread on a plate. Now sprinkle a little fried thickened milk, ground sugar on it. Sprinkle cardamom powder on top and decorate with cherries. Cut the other apple into pieces in the shape of flowers and decorate it separately. People will take pieces of apple or 'fruit sweet' according to their preference. You can also make a well dressed boy armed with spoons with the other apple and make the table look more attractive insisting you to eat. You may think of any new decoration and see how there is a spurt in the demand for this fruit sweet, instead of sweets like *Gulab Jamun* and *Halwa*.

Tip off

An apple a day keeps the doctor away.

Decorated Banana Dish

Bananas are not only healthy but they are delicious too.

Banana Dish

Ingredients

2 bananas
salt (to taste)
pepper
black salt (to taste)

Method

Put the bananas in a beautiful, coloured wicker or plastic basket. Peel the bananas for eating. Slit them from the centre lengthwise and stuff spices (salt, black salt and black pepper). Decorate them in circles and place small salt and pepper cellars in the middle. Or if more bananas are needed, peel them and decorate them straight or in angular position on a long small tray and keep salt and pepper cellars separately. Plate, knife, fork and bouquet of flowers in a basket will add to the attraction. Taking two bananas for breakfast is healthy and an easily affordable way of getting nutrition. Remember not to add spices like salt and pepper to bananas if they are to be taken with milk.

Tip off

Bananas are rich source of potassium.

Decorated Cottage Cheese Salad

Cottage cheese (paneer) is white, soft and tasty. We can either cook it in gravy or eat it as salad.

Cottage Cheese Salad

Ingredients

To make cheese:
½ litre milk
1 lemon

For salad:
1 radish
2 carrots
some lettuce leaves

Method

Instead of buying cottage cheese (paneer) from the market, make it at home by curdling milk. Squeeze the juice of one lemon in ½ litre boiling milk or add a piece of gram sized citric acid to curdle milk. Strain through a piece of muslin and hang for some time. After all the water is drained, mash it with hand, add salt and put under a heavy stone. After an hour, it will be a hard slice of *paneer* or cottage cheese. Cut it in various forms of flowers and leaves and decorate on a plate. Garnish and decorate with radish, carrot and lettuce. Cut radish and carrot also in various shapes of flowers and leaves. Cottage cheese is saltish. It may be eaten with lemon juice sprinkled on top, plain or with salad. It can also be served as sandwich filling by placing between two slices of bread. Cottage cheese is an essential source of protein for those who do not take eggs for breakfast.

Tip off

Cottage cheese (paneer) is low in calories than the processed cheese.

Sprouted Beans

Sprouted beans can be eaten at breakfast as a substitute for eggs or cottage cheese.

Sprouted Beans

Ingredients

50 gms whole *moong dal*
20 gms dried peas
20 grams gram
1 lemon
salt (to taste)
pepper (to taste)

For decoration (optional):
onion rings
green chillies
lettuce leaves

Method

Soak whole *moong*, dried peas and gram for 24 hours (1 day). Then tie them up in a cloth and hang them for the next 24 hours. In summer, keep on sprinkling water on the tied bundle of beans. They will sprout on the third day.

Sprinkle salt, pepper and lemon juice on the sprouted beans and eat them raw for breakfast. It is a healthier way of eating them. If you cannot take it raw, sauté in a little ghee or oil and steam a little bit. Decorate on the plate with lettuce, lemon, onion rings, green chillies before eating.

Tip off

Sprouted beans form a good and healthy diet, rich in proteins and vitamin C.

Porridge

Milk and Porridge is a common dish for breakfast, but a decorated plate of it makes all the difference.

Porridge

Ingredients

½ cup porridge
2 cups milk
sugar (to taste)

For garnishing:
chopped almonds
chopped cashew
pounded cardamom seeds

Method

Make porridge of good coarse wheat at home. Sift to separate the flour from the upper thick crust and use the porridge that remains after sifting. If it is to be taken with milk, roast it on low fire without ghee. Then add water and cook. When tender, add sugar and milk as per taste and serve. Garnish with chopped almonds, cashews or peanuts or with pounded cardamom seeds. It has to be decorated with powdered cardamom to look more alluring. Milk and porridge can be mixed together while eating.

If porridge has to be eaten as a tasty dish, without milk, roast porridge on a low fire in ghee till pink in colour. Add hot water and cook till tender. Add sugar and keep on low flame for five minutes. Take off from the fire and serve on a plate like *halwa* garnished with chopped dry fruits, cardamom seeds and cherry (optional).

Tip off

Porridge is a palatable and nutritious dish for breakfast.

Vegetable Cutlets

The base for the cutlets may be potato but you may add as many vegetables in it as you like.

Vegetable Cutlets

Ingredients

250 gms potatoes
100 gms shelled peas
2 carrots
1 tomato
2 onions
salt (to taste)
garam masala (mixture of hot, grounded Indian spices)
green chillies
ghee
tomato sauce
1 tbsp flour

Method

Boil, peel and mash potatoes. Boil shelled peas and small pieces of carrot. Peel tomato and take out the pulp. Chop green chillies and one onion finely.

Mix everything together. After adding salt and garam masala. Then make longish flat cakes using the palm of your hand. Dissolve one big spoon of flour in water. (If eggs can be used, use one beaten egg instead). Dip the cakes first in flour or egg batter. Then coat with bread crumbs. Press them with hands to shape them properly and fry in hot ghee on a flattish pan or *tawa*. Tawa should be heavy and not too shallow. Otherwise fry them on low fire after the sides are red, so that the inside is also fried well. When ready, serve hot with onion, carrot, cucumber rings decorated on a plate and tomato sauce.

Tip off

Bread crumbs can also be made with dried bread slices.

Potato Bonda and Cottage Cheese

This is a delicious dish which is a favourite of old and young alike.

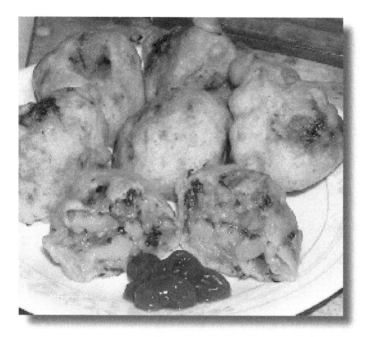

Potato Bonda amd Cottage Cheese

Ingredients

200 gms potato
4 tbsp gram flour
1 onion
2 green chillies
salt (to taste)
1 tsp *amchur*
½ *garam masala*
1 tsp ghee.

Method

Boil, peel and mash potatoes. Mix chopped green chillies, chopped onion, salt, *garam masala* and *amchur*. Knead the mixture and make small balls.

Make a thin batter of gram flour. Add salt, chopped coriander and a pinch of red chilli powder. Coat the balls of the mixture with this batter and fry in ghee. Salty Potato Bonda – a tea time snack is ready. Pieces of cottage cheese or *paneer* can also be coated with this batter and fried, or fry these pieces without batter on a *tawa* in a little ghee. Fry only one side and let the other side remain white. Serve them with *chutney*.

Tip off
Potato Bondas are also known as Batata Vadas.

Balls of Moong Dal

This is a nutritious snack which is rich in proteins.

Balls of Moong Dal

Ingredients

100 gms whole *moong dal* (split green gram)
Chopped coriander
½ tsp coriander
a pinch of *amchur* (dried mango powder)
¼ tsp *garam masala*
salt and red chillie powder (as per taste)

Methods

Clean whole *moong dal* or split green gram and soak it in water overnight. Remove the skin in the morning and grind to a fine paste with a grinding stone, to make good, fluffy, soft balls.

Now add salt, red chilli powder, chopped coriander, coriander powder, a pinch of *amchur*, *garam masala* to this batter and whip till frothy. Spices should not be too much and the batter should be whipped well.

Heat oil or ghee in a vessel, make small balls with your hands and fry them in a frying pan.

These almond-sized balls should be fluffy, soft balls. Serve them hot with mint *chutney* or tomato sauce.

Tip off

Mangod is a very small ball of moong dal which is not fried but sun-dried. When many of these are prepared together, packed in the market, they are called *Mangodi*.

Gram Flour Bhajias

As the first rain of monsoon falls, *bhajias* along with hot tea make the day worthwhile.

Gram Flour Bhajias

Ingredients

1 cup gram flour
potato
brinjal
cauliflower
onion
spinach
salt (to taste)
chillies
fennel
coriander leaves
pomegranate seeds or *amchur*
oil or ghee (for frying)

Method

Cut potato, brinjal and onion in rings. Chop the spinach finely. Also chop the coriander leaves and green chillies also. Cut the cauliflower in very thin slices.

Make a batter of gram flour, which should be of medium consistency. Add salt, chopped green chillies, red chilli powder as required, *amchur*, ½ small spoon fennel and whip,. Dip the vegetable rings and slices in this batter and fry in oil or ghee. If the vegetables do not cook fully the first time, then press the *Bhajias* with your hands or a spatula and fry again. Serve hot with mint *chutney* or tomato sauce.

Tip off

Bhajia is a popular snack in North India and it is liked by everyone these days. Besides being a snack with a tingling taste, it is also quite filling like *parathas* and *puris*. But it is more healthy if taken in small quantities. So eat only a few pieces with tea or put them in between two slices of bread and eat like a sandwich, with *chutney*.

Salty Vermicelli

Sweet Vermicelli is a common dish in most of the households. Make Salty Vermicelli in the same way and serve hot for breakfast.

Salty Vermicelli

Ingredients

vermicelli
onion,
cumin seeds
cloves
black cardamom
green coriander
cottage cheese (paneer)

Method

Cut onion into thin slices. Heat ghee in a vessel and fry the onion till red. Add cumin seeds, black cardamom, cloves and vermicelli. Fry a bit on low heat. Then add hot water, salt and cover with a lid. Water should be just enough for the vermicelli to soak and rise. They will break or become pasty, if cooked for too long in too much water. So use very little water right from the beginning. If necessary, sprinkle water later. Make the flame high after adding water. Then lower the flame completely after one boil and cook, covered with a lid. The vermicelli is now ready after cooking for three minutes. It may be cooked with shelled peas, or groundnuts if desired.

Spread the vermicelli on a flat plate like rice. Garnish with chopped green coriander and grated cottage cheese (paneer). Salads and *chutney* can also be served with it. You can also eat it with mint *chutney* and tomato sauce.

Tip off

Vermicelli is made of semolina, hence it is very nutritious.

Stuffed Toasts

Stuffed toasts are made with mixed vegetables, potatoes, egg omelette or minced meat. These crisp toasts are very filling and tasty tea time snacks and can be eaten for lunch also.

Stuffed Toasts

Ingredients

10 or 12 bread slices
250 gms potatoes
other vegetables
50gms shelled peas (boiled)
1 tomato
1 onion
spices
ghee or butter
(can be prepared with boiled eggs,
omelette or mined meat)

Method

Boil, peel and mash the potatoes, If other vegetables like cauliflower, carrot, beans, etc. have to be used, cut them into small pieces and boil them once with shelled peas. Heat one big spoon of ghee in a frying pan and fry chopped onion. Add the mashed potatoes, boiled vegetables, salt, chopped green chillies, and a pinch of *garam masala*. Stir and take off the flame.

Grease the toaster with one small spoon of ghee or butter. Put one slice of bread in the toaster, spread the mixture on it, cover it with another slice. Now put one small spoon of ghee or butter on top of the second slice of bread. Close the toaster and put on the stove or gas. Toast it on both the sides by turning. Take out when red. It takes a little time to cook the first toast. But once the toaster is heated up, subsequent toasts are ready very fast.

Put them on a plate and garnish with tomato sauce and green coriander, or wrap them up in a paper without any decoration. You can also take them to office or for a journey.

Tip off
To make this dish more healthy, use brown bread instead of normal flour bread.

Potato-Bread Rolls

These crispy, yummy Bread Rolls can be given to children in their school tiffin or lunch box.

Potato-Bread Rolls

Ingredients

10 bread slices
250 gms potato
green coriander
green chillies
1 tomato
1 onion
salt (to taste)
garam masala (to taste)
ghee, oil or butter (for frying)

Method

Boil, peel and mash the potatoes. Take water in a deep plate. Dip two slices of bread in water and squeeze out the water. Knead with potatoes. Mix salt, chopped green chillies, chopped coriander, 1 small spoon *garam masala*, finely chopped onion and mashed tomato pulp. Juice of half a lemon can be used instead of tomato.

Now dip the other eight slices of bread in water one by one. Press with your palms to drain out water. Put the potato filling with spoon on each slice, roll and give a longish, round shape with your hands. Now, deep fry each roll in heated ghee, oil or butter one by one till moderately red. Serve on a long tray-like plate with salads, *chutney* or tomato sauce. Decorate with flowers cut out of tomato and onion. Green chillies and radish flowers may also be used for garnishing.

Tip off

Round cakes and triangular samosas can also be made with wet bread slices, stuffed with potato mixture.

Vegetarian Omelette

Vegetarian Omelette can be served to people who do not eat eggs, but are on a breakfast table with others to whom egg omelette are to be served.

Vegetarian Omelette

Ingredients

¼ cup gram flour
1 cup rice flour
1 big onion
green coriander
green chillies
turmeric and
red chilli powder
ghee, oil or butter

Method

Chop the onion, green chillies and green coriander finely. Mix the gram flour and rice flour and dissolve to make a batter. Add chopped onion, coriander, chillies and salt, along with turmeric, red chilli powder and whip.

Heat the ghee, oil or butter in a frying pan or *tawa* and spread the thick batter evenly on it with a large round spoon. Now set the edges with this spoon only. Turn with a spatula, sprinkle ghee, oil or butter on top and fry. Serve hot, decorated with salads, sauce or chutney. Tomato rings, cucumber and radish flowers may also be used to decorate the dish.

Tip off

To make it more nutritions, you may add any grated vegetables like bottlegourd, cottage cheese, etc. to the batter.

Egg Penguin

Eggs are eaten in many forms. This is one of them.

Egg Penguin

Ingredients

6 eggs
250 gms potato
2 spoons chocolate powder
or cocoa powder
8 cloves
butter
lettuce leaves
salt (to taste)
black pepper (to taste)

Method

Hard boil eggs and peel. Keep four eggs intact and cut rings out of the two eggs with a cutter or knife. Boil the potatoes and peel. Add salt, black pepper, cocoa chocolate powder and mash well. Coat the whole eggs with this mixture and shape them like penguins, as illustrated. The belly in front should be left uncovered and white.

Make four birds this way and insert two cloves in each for the eyes. Rub with butter and bake in a moderate oven. While decorating them on a plate, place them on lettuce leaves previously cut like flat feet. Can be served with boiled egg rings too.

Tip off

This egg penguin preparation will be specially interesting for children's party. Make as many penguins as there are invitees.

Boiled Egg Jester

Here is another fun recipe of eggs.

Boiled Egg Jester

Ingredients

6 boiled eggs
rings of cucumber, radish, onion,
tomato

Method

Place the hard boiled, peeled eggs on thick rings of cucumber, radish, or tomato. Make eyes, nose, eyebrows, moustaches, etc., on these eggs with salad dressings mixed with chocolate or cocoa. Take a bit of salad dressing on a spoon separately, and add red edible colouring to it. Now put dots all over the faces of the eggs to look like jesters. Cut thick rings from small red tomatoes from both the sides. Empty them from the centre and place them on the heads of these jesters, to look like caps. Pointed caps made from onion skins can also be used. These jesters will be highly appreciated in a children's party.

Tip off

Egg is a part of our daily diet barring the strictly vegetarians. Boiled egg, poached egg, fried egg, omelette, French toasts, sandwich, egg curry and so many other preparations of eggs, are used by us almost everyday.

Making an Omelette

Egg omelette is as popular in breakfast as tea or coffee.

Omelette

Ingredients

2 eggs

chilli powder, salt, *garam masala* (to taste)

1 chopped green chilli

1 finely chopped onion

ghee/oil/butter

Methods

➤ Break open two eggs.

➤ Whip it well, the white and yellow of eggs the first separately and then together. Add chillies, salt, *garam masala*, finely chopped green chillies and finely chopped onion, etc., as per taste.

➤ Put ghee, oil or butter in a frying pan and put the mixture, spreading it with a spatula in a round manner. When done on one side, fold it and do the other side. Then bring down from the fire. It should not be overcooked.

➤ And here's your omelette, ready to be eaten.

Tip off

A few drops of fresh milk added to the egg batter while whipping will make the omelette soft and fluffy.

Stuffed Eggs

This dish has a stuffy name but it is as light as it can be.

Stuffed Eggs

Ingredients

7 eggs
½ cup minced meat or (paneer)
½ cup grated cottage cheese
2 tbsp of tomato sauce
1 tbsp of chilli sauce
1 big or medium onion
butter / oil / ghee
coriander leaves
green chillies
butter or ghee (to taste)

Method

Hard boil six eggs. Peel and cut into halves lengthwise. Take out the yellow portion with the tip of a knife. Put ghee or butter in a frying pan and fry the finely chopped coriander leaves, green chillies, salt and grated cottage cheese. Mix the chillie sauce and tomato sauce, stir and take off from the fire. Now mash the yellow of the eggs and mix with it

Fill up the hollows in eggs with this mixture carefully till the top. You can use mined meat insead of cottage cheese.

Whip the remaining eggs, add a pinch of salt and pepper. Grease the baking dish with butter. Dip each piece of boiled egg in whipped egg and place it straight in the baking dish. Now bake them in a moderately heated oven. Decorate these stuffed eggs on a plate with salads. Pieces of fried meat or egg placed on cucumber and radish slices can also be used for decoration.

Tip off

This preparation of eggs is also called Devil Eggs or *Egg Devils*.

French Toast

This dish may be made sweet or salty depending upon your taste.

French Toast

Ingredients

6 bread slices
2 eggs
200 ml milk
sugar (to taste)
ghee (for frying)

Method

Break eggs and separate the yellow yolk from the white.

Whip some milk with the yellow of the eggs and add sugar as per your taste. Heat ghee in a shallow vessel or pan (tawa). Cut bread slices into triangles (12 pieces). Dip each slice into the egg and milk mixture and fry on the *tawa*. Keep on turning till brown on both sides. Decorate on a plate in the shape of a flower and put cashew nuts in the centre like the pollen. To make it salty, just substitute sugar with salt and continue with the same process.

Tip off

To separate the yolk and the egg white, you may use a separator.

Mixed Vegetable Pickle

This recipe is for the mango season.

Mixed Vegetable Pickle

Ingredients

1½ kg of raw mango
300 ml vinegar
500 gms jack fruit
250 gms mustard oil
250 gms green chillies
15 gms jaggery
250 gms lime
250 gms ground salt
250 gms sour berries (karaunda)
250 gms onion
25 gms of turmeric powder
30 gms garlic
50 gms red chillies
60 gms ginger
25 gms black pepper
cumin seeds
cinnamon
glacial acetic acid

Method

Grind together the ginger, garlic and onions. Peel the jackfruit and cut into pieces. Slit the green chillies. Wash, wipe, dry and grate the mangoes (may be used peeled or unpeeled). Cut lemon into four pieces. Grind the spices and keep them ready for use.

Boil the jackfruit pieces once and spread them on cloth to dry. It is better to cook them in steam. Now heat oil in a vessel. When it starts smoking, lower the flame and fry onions, garlic and ginger. Add turmeric, red chilli powder and cinnamon. Now put the pounded jaggery (gud). When the jaggery starts giving bubbles, take the vessel off the flame. Add all the cut vegetables and whole sour berries, salt and black pepper. Turn and toss well. Then add the vinegar. Add two small spoons of Glacial Acetic Acid in the end and store in a clay jar. Put out in the sun for three to four days for preserving. This five hued sweet-sour pickle can be preserved for a long time.

Tip off

In winter, spices, oil and salt in the same proportion can be mixed with 2 kg of cauliflower, carrots, turnips and lemons. Since there will be no sour berries and mangoes in this, do not forget to add 125 gms of mustard seeds for saute in oil.

Sweet-Sour Chutney

This *chutney* has a special flavour which enhances the taste of the main dish.

Sweet-Sour Chutney

Ingredients

2 bananas
½ tsp ground black pepper
1 apple
½ cup tamarind
1 cup sugar
25 gms raisins (kismis)
4 large cardamom
2 tbsps oil
1 tsp ground fried cumin seeds
asafoetida, mustard (rai) (to taste)
½ tsp ground *saunth* (dried ginger powder)
2 tsps grated coconut
2 tsps arrowroot

Method

Clean the tamarind and soak in a glass or a stainless steel vessel of water for two to three hours. Squeeze the juice and strain. Cut an apple into small pieces. Cut the rings of ripe but firm bananas. Clean the raisins. Grind coarsely the cardamom seeds. Heat two tablespoons of oil in a stainless steel vessel. Saute asafoetida and mustard seeds. Add the tamarind water. Mix the arrowroot dissolved in water. After it boils, add one cup of sugar and cook till the *chutney's* consistency is thick, stirring constantly. Add the raisins while cooking, so that they puff up a little. Then add the pieces of bananas and apples. Remove after one minute and add the grounded mint, *saunth*, fried cumin seeds, black pepper, grated coconut, cardamom powder and salt as per taste. A very tasty sweet-sour *chutney* is now ready to be served with salty delicacies and *chaat*.

Tip off

Refrigerate this *chutney* so that it may be used for a longer period.

Tomato Sauce

This thin consistency sauce made of pure tomatoes is known as *tomato ketchup* also. Tomato sauce of thick consistency, sold in shops, is not made of pure tomatoes. Vegetable pulp and colouring is added to it. If you wish to make a cheaper sauce of thick consistency, pumpkin pulp can also be added to the sauce, while being cooked. But pure tomato ketchup is tastier and has better food values.

Tomato Sauce

Ingredients

2½ or 3 kg large red tomatoes
250 or 300 gms sugar
125 or 150 gms onion
2-3 inch piece ginger
15 flakes of garlic
10 gms red chilli powder or grounded green chillies
40 gms salt
10 gms *garam masala*
1½ or 2 gms sodium benzoate
25 to 50 gms vinegar

Method

Wash and cut the tomatoes and put on fire in a stainless steel utensil. Grind to paste the onions, garlic, ginger and mix with the tomatoes. After the tomatoes become soft, crush the mixture and strain to separate the seeds and skin. Now put the strained juice on fire again. Add 1/3 of the sugar to it. Boil the *garam masala* and red chilli in the little water in a separate utensil. Crush, strain and mix the tomato juice. Cook for 10 to 12 minutes and add the rest of the sugar and cook again. Put on a plate to see if the sauce is ready. If the water separates on the plate, it needs more cooking. Add salt and take off from the fire. Put Sodium Benzoate and Vinegar on top. A pinch of red food colouring may also be added, if desired. Now fill up the bottles with the sauce, while still hot. Close the lid and seal with wax after it cools down.

Tip off

The tomato sauce should be made during the season when tomatoes are cheap and preserved for the rest of the year. Then cheap and pure sauce can be enjoyed throughout the year. Sodium Benzoate is a preservative, so it can be stored for a long time.

Tomato Chutney

This *chutney* can be eaten with *paranthas*.

Tomato Chutney

Ingredients

2 kg tomato
500 gms sugar
10 gms red chilli powder
10 gms *garam masala*
30 gms salt
5-10 gms pepper
5 gms black cumin seeds
2 inch piece ginger
2 tsps glacial acetic acid

Method

Wash and cut the tomatoes and cook in a stainless steel vessel. Add the ground ginger. When fully cooked, pass through a stainless steel or aluminium sieve to separate the skin, the juice and the pulp till it attains a thick consistency. Add sugar and black cumin seeds. Cook for about ten minutes. Then add the red chilli powder, *garam masala* and salt.

Put on a plate to see whether the water separates or not. Take off from fire after it is cooked and add the glacial Acetic Acid. Then pour this thick *chutney* while hot in bottles with broad mouths. If desired, it can be tempered with mustard seeds, asafoetida, ground onions and garlic in a little oil. A few raisins (kismis) can also be added to make it more tasty.

Tip off
Those who do not like the flavour of garlic and onions can skip adding them in the *chutney*.

Chocolate Sauce

This chocolate sauce may be poured over a cold ice cream.

Chocolate Sauce

Ingredients

½ or 1 cup cocoa powder
a pinch of salt
a cup of sugar
vanilla essence
1 cup water
1 tsp of cream or butter

Method

Add the half or one cup of cocoa powder in one cup of water. Cook till the mixture is thick in consistency. Add a pinch of salt and a cup of sugar and cook to thicken it more. Now the vanilla essence may be added along with a teaspoon of fresh cream or butter.

Your lip-smacking chocolate sauce is ready to be poured over a cold ice cream or custard to make it really tasty.

Tip off
The amount of sugar may vary as per taste in this sauce.

Lemon Sauce

Lemon sauce has a tingy taste and flavour, but very healthy to eat, rich in vitamins.

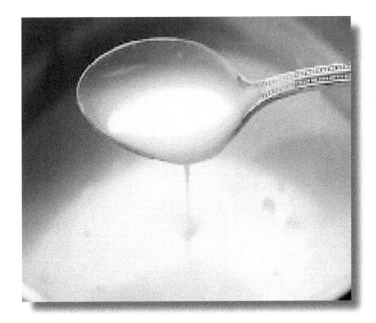

Lemon Sauce

Ingredients

1 tsp cornflour
4 tsps water
½ or ¾ cup sugar, as per taste
salt (to taste)
1 tsp lemon rind
juice of one lemon
a pinch of nutmeg (jaiphal)
powder

Method

Dissolve one spoon of cornflour in about four spoons of water. Then add to one cup of boiling water and stir. Add half or three-fourth cup of sugar, salt and nutmeg (jaiphal). Add one spoon of finely chopped lemon rind. Take off from the fire and add the juice of one lemon. Some essence can also be added. It can be tempered too, if desired.

Tip off

This sauce is rich in vitamin C, and is a health food.

Mayonnaise

Mayonnaise may be used in making fillings for sandwiches or used as a dip.

Mayonnaise

Ingredients

2 eggs
1 tsp sugar
½ tsp mustard paste
½ cup vinegar
2 tsps of lemon juice
1 cup salad oil

Method

Beat the yolks of two eggs gradually, adding salt, a small spoon of sugar and ground chillies to it. Add half a spoon of mustard seeds also. Now keep one to one and half cups of salad oil, half a cup of vinegar and two spoons of lemon juice separately. Add these drop by drop, turn by turn and keep on stirring. After the Mayonnaise becomes thick, one spoon of oil can also be added. Lastly add one cup of boiling water and whip till it becomes frothy like the fresh cream. Before serving, cool in the refrigerator.

Tip off

For eggless mayonnaise, do not put eggs in this recipe.

Booster Sauce

Booster Sauce has a sweet and sour flavour. It has an altogether different and unique taste.

Booster Sauce

Ingredients

5 cloves
1 inch piece of ginger
4 flakes of garlic
1 cup vinegar
½ or 1 tsp black pepper
¼ or ½ tsp red chilli powder
some raisins (kismis)

Method

Wet grind about five cloves, one inch piece of ginger and four flakes of garlic with a little vinegar. Caramelise one-fourth cup of sugar till deep red. Add the spices, one cup vinegar, salt, half teaspoon of black pepper and half or one-fourth spoon of red chilli powder. Boil all these for about five minutes. Strain and preserve in a bottle. Raisins may also be added to it.

Tip off

If fresh ginger is not available, then dry ginger powder (saunth) can also be used in the sauce.

White Sauce

White sauce is easy to make and good to eat.

White Sauce

Ingredients

1 tbsp cornflour
1 tbsp salad oil
1 cup milk
salt (to taste)
pinch of black pepper

Method

Mix one tablespoon of cornflour, salt and a pinch of ground black pepper. Heat a tablespoon of salad oil and add cornflour to it. Cook on low fire for about four to five minutes, stirring all the time. Keep stirring. Then add a cup of hot milk till it thickens gradually.

Now put the leftover water of boiled vegetables and the meat pieces or chicken pieces in the middle. Break an egg on top and take the heater to the dining table.

Tip off

White sauce, soya sauce and chilli sauce are used mainly for Chinese dishes. If you are a vegetarian, avoid the use of eggs, meat or chicken pieces.

Mango Jam

Children love eating mango jam as a spread on bread slices.

Mango Jam

Ingredients

1 kg ripe mangoes
2½ kg sugar
4 gms citric acid

Method

Peel and grate the mangoes used for *murabbas*. Soak the grated mangoes in lime water for 10 minutes. Wash and spread on a cloth. Make a syrup with sugar, one and half times more than the weight of mangoes. After boiling the syrup once, add the grated mangoes and cook till tender. To check whether the jam is fully cooked or not, put one drop of it on a plate. If the drop falls like a round ball without spilling on the sides, the jam is ready. Add citric acid to the syrup (in the proportion of one kilo to four grams,) while being cooked.

Now fill up the hot jam in bottles cleaned earlier and kept ready. Leave them uncovered till cool. Then cover them with lids and seal. To seal, melt wax in a utensil and put the closed bottle (wide-mouthed bottles should be used to store jam) upside down in it. Open one bottle at a time for use.

Tip off

If you like your mango jam very sweet, then make sure that the mangoes you use are not of sweet-sour variety.

Apple Jam

For those, who do not have time to munch an apple can spread this jam on their toasts and get the goodness of an apple.

Ingredients

1 kg apples
2½ kg sugar
4 gms citric acid
2 % salt water

Apple Jam

Method

Apple jam is made and preserved in the same way as grated mangoes, except grated apples should not be soaked in lime water like grated mangoes. Apples should be soaked in 2 per cent salt water, to prevent it from turning black. Then put them straight in the sugar syrup and cook. Citric acid should be added in the same proportion, as in a mango jam.

Tip off

Apple is rich in iron and very essential for people of all ages. An apple a day, keeps the doctor away!

Amla Murabba

This *murabba* is very nutritious and healthy if you eat this on an empty stomach, first thing in the morning.

Amla Murabba

Ingredients

2 kg *amlas* or Indian goose berries
1 cup lemon juice
100 gms crystal sugar
1 litre of water
sugar to make one-string syrup
pinch of cardamom powder
2-3 leaves of saffron

Method

Soak about two kilos of good, ripe, stain-free, big *amlas* (Indian goose berries) in plain water for two or three days. Take out and dry on a cloth and pierce with a fork. Then soak them again for another three days in lime water. Take out on the fourth day and rinse in clean water. Soak about 100 gms, crystal sugar (mishri) in one litre of water and boil the *amlas* in this water. When half-cooked, take out and spread on a clean cloth.

Now make the sugar syrup double the quantity of the *amlas*. Put the *amlas* after the first boil and cook. Take off from the fire after ten minutes and keep aside for a day. Then put on the flame again and cook till the syrup is of one-string consistency. Take off from the fire and let it cool. Sprinkle cardamom powder and saffron.

Tip off

This *murabba* does not need any preservative. Store in jars and put silver wrapper, while serving.

Carrot Murabba

This *murabba* is good for the eyes as carrots are a rich source of vitamin A, which is very good for our eyes.

Carrot Murabba

Ingredients

2 kg carrots
sugar syrup of one-string consistency
6 gms citric acid
cardamom powder
silver wrapper for decoration (optional)

Method

Clean about two kilos of thick carrots. Scrape and wash the carrots. Cut them into large pieces for *Murabba*. Cut the thicker ends into two pieces from the middle and the lower ends can be left as it is. Give these pieces one boil in water. Take off from the fire and spread on a clean cloth. Pierce here and there with a stainless steel fork.

Now make the sugar syrup, one and a half times more in quantity than the carrot pieces. Add the carrot pieces to the syrup after it boils once and cook for about ten minutes. Then take off from the fire and keep aside for a day. Next day, put it on the flame again and cook till the syrup is of about one string consistency. Add the citric acid or lemon juice and take off from the flame. Grind the cardamoms and sprinkle on top. Store in a jar and decorate with silver wrapper while serving.

Tip off

For carrot *murabba*, the carrots should be thick, but not knotty from inside.

Strawberry Jelly

Housewives often complain about imperfect jellies made with fresh fruits. But now packets of jelly crystals are available in plenty and it is easy to set the jellies with them. These jelly crystals are available in various flavours of orange, strawberry, pineapple, etc.

Strawberry Jelly

Ingredients

1 cup jelly crystals
¼ or ½ cup sugar
1½ cups hot water
1½ cup strawberry juice
some crepe wafers (optional)
(for decoration)

Method

Add one-third to half cup of sugar for one cup of jelly crystals. Add three cups of hot water (or 1 1/2 cups of hot water and 1 ½ cups of fruit juice instead, as convenient) and whip well. Some fresh fruit juice should be added according to the flavour of the crystals, like orange crystals should be mixed with orange juice and pineapple crystals with pineapple juice. Refrigerate it after whipping. Coloured, transparent, well-set jelly will be ready in two to three hours. Decorate with crepe wafers, if readily available.

Tip off

If you like fruit pieces inside the jelly, then you may add them on top of the jelly as a topping while serving.

Squash

First of all, know the difference between a *squash* and *sherbat*. *Sherbat* has more sugar and squash has more juice. Because sugar itself is a preservative, there is no need to add any chemical preservative to the *sherbat*. Because squash has less sugar and more of juice, preservative has to be used for storing it for a long time.

Recipes for these two kinds of squashes have been evolved by the Indian Council of Agricultural Research (ICAR) and can be prepared at home.

Lemon Squash

Ingredients

1 litre fruit juice
1 kg sugar
½ litre lemon juice
2 gms Potassium Metabisulphite
and juice of fruit rinds or
essence for flavour

Method

Formula 1: Extract the juice of six, large oranges. Strain the juice either through a piece of muslin or stainless steel strainer, so that the seeds are separated from the fibres and the pulp. Boil the lemon juice and sugar together (water should not be used). Strain after one boil and let it cool. Add the strained juice of orange. Now add a few drops of orange essence or juice of orange rind for flavouring. A little yellow food colouring may also be added. But it is preferable to avoid it. Dissolve Potassium Metabisulphite in a little water and add to it. This works as a preservative. Now fill up the squash after cooling, in sterilized bottles.

Formula 2: Extract the orange juice and strain as before. Boil adding sugar, citric acid and water. Strain after boiling twice. Cool and add the juice, essence and the food colouring, if preferred. In the end, dissolve the Potassium Metabisulphite in water and add as before. Refrigerate the squash bottle or keep it outside, as you prefer. Shake the bottle, every time you want to use the squash. *In summer afternoons, these squashes are a treat in itself!*

Tip off

You can make squashes of other juicy fruits, such as oranges, mangoes, grapes or pineapples in the same way.